By Taijah Cox-Armstrong
Designed and Edited by: BOURGIE Branding

Built for Real Women, Driven by Hustle

© 2025 Taijah Cox-Armstrong. All rights reserved.

No part of this publication may be reproduced, distributed, or transmitted in any form or by any means, electronic or mechanical, including photocopying, recording, or other methods, without the prior written permission of the author, except as permitted by applicable copyright law.

For permissions requests, contact Taijah Cox-Armstrong: taijahcoxarmstrong@gmail.com.

ISBN: 978-1-7387254-2-7

Taijah Cox-Armstrong asserts the moral right to be identified as the author of this work.

My Journey: From Multiple Jobs to Multiple Businesses

Growing up, I was always a passionate person, but it wasn't until I got involved in community work that I truly discovered my purpose. I can't pinpoint exactly where that passion came from, but it always felt natural, like something ingrained in me. I quickly realized that my passion was rooted in helping others—whether it was a specific community, group, or individual, I wanted to make a positive impact in people's lives.

When people ask how or why I began working in the community, my honest answer is simple: it just felt right. Every time I was able to help someone, it felt almost like an out-of-body experience. In those moments, I felt deeply connected to something larger than myself. Hearing people's stories and knowing that I could make even a small difference in their lives fueled my desire to do more and more within the community.

But one of the most frequent questions I get asked is:

"Who ARE you? Who IS Taijah?"

Hi, my name is Taijah Cox-Armstrong, and I'm a Black woman, entrepreneur, community leader, and changemaker. I was born in Toronto and raised in Brampton, Ontario, where my journey in community leadership began at a young age.

It all started with a role at a non-profit organization called One Voice, One Team, in downtown Brampton.

Every day on my way to work, I would pass by a homeless community near the local 7-11. And every day, I asked myself, "What can I do to help?"

I felt a strong pull to do something, but at that time, I also knew my resources were limited. Still, I couldn't ignore the need. So, I took action—small but meaningful. I organized my first donation drive. I created a flyer, reached out to my friends and family, set up a table, and went downtown to hand out the items I had collected. That day, I felt something shift inside me. I realized I had found my passion. Or so I thought.

At that point, I believed my calling was to support the homeless community, so I organized two more donation drives. Each drive deepened my sense of purpose, but it also opened my eyes to a bigger truth: the more I gave, the more I realized there was always more to be done, and my journey of service was just beginning.

Then, June 2020 hit, and the rise of protests and advocacy for the Black community reached an all-time high. The movement felt deeply personal to me—being a young Black woman myself, I knew I had to contribute in some way. I wanted to not only support the cause but also make a meaningful, lasting impact for the Black community.

So I asked myself, *How can I use my talents and skills to advocate for this movement? How can I truly make a difference?*

It wasn't just about standing in solidarity—it was about taking action. I knew that my journey wasn't just about helping individuals on a personal level; it was about fighting for systemic change, raising awareness, and uplifting my community in ways that went beyond just donations and drives.

I was ready to step up and leverage everything I had learned to help amplify the voices of those who needed to be heard, to create real change in our community, and to fight for justice, equality, and opportunity.

That's when I decided to step up and lead. I co-organized a rally called *"Peel's March for Justice"*, aimed at addressing the systemic racism embedded within the Peel District School Board. I remember that day vividly—the passion I felt as we marched down Hurontario, from the Peel police station to the Peel District School Board, chanting and demanding change. It was powerful. But even in that moment, something inside me still felt incomplete. I wanted to do more. I wanted to be part of something bigger, something that would leave a lasting impact.

So, I began sitting on panels with the Peel police, and even had discussions with Mayor Patrick Brown, sharing my perspectives on the issues at hand. I took part in interviews, hoping my voice would inspire others to take action. But still, I didn't feel like I was doing enough. I needed to dig deeper, to create something that could empower the next generation.

That's when I wrote my book:

"I Will Make a Difference"

It's a children's activity booklet for kids ages 7-13 that teaches them about their identity, the power of their voice, and how they can make a meaningful difference in the world around them. It was my way of giving young people the tools to shape their own future, to understand that they have a voice that matters, and that they can create change—starting now.

Today, that book has evolved into my incredible business:

"Change4Thought"

Through this platform, I now have the opportunity to go into schools, non-profit organizations, and camps to host workshops based around my book. It's been an amazing journey—one that began with passion and has grown into a mission to teach kids how to use their voices to create change around the issues they care about.

When I look at how my passion for helping others has grown, I see it in many different forms. It's me organizing and hosting networking events designed to create spaces for women, youth, and entrepreneurs to connect and support each other. It's me hosting job fairs to help young people—just like I once was—navigate the often difficult path to employment. It's me offering free workshops for youth, where they can explore their identities, discover their passions, and understand that they have the power to shape their future.

This journey has been about more than just giving back. It's about creating opportunities for others to rise, and empowering them to realize their potential. Every step I take in this work—whether it's through workshops, events, or writing—is a step toward creating a world where everyone has a voice, a chance, and the tools they need to make a difference.

My journey, however, wasn't easy. To fund a lot of my initiatives, I had to work multiple jobs.

In high school, I worked at Mary Brown's and Canada's Wonderland, and later took on jobs in warehouses, youth organizations, and pretty much anywhere I could find work. I was juggling multiple jobs to keep my community initiatives alive, but there were days when I was literally using my last dollar to fund a project. The weight of it all started to take its toll, and eventually, I reached a point of burnout.

That's when I realized I needed to turn to my community for support. I signed myself up for a free business class offered by Delta Family Resource Center, and that was a game changer. In that class, I started learning how to truly maximize my resources and how to build a sustainable business from my passions. It was there that I realized I didn't have to choose between my work and my community—it was possible to merge the two in a way that supported both.

If there's one piece of advice I would give, it's this:

"take the time to educate yourself, to learn about the business world, and to understand the tools and resources available to you. Knowledge is power!"

Empowering yourself with the right knowledge is what gives you the ability to turn your dreams into a sustainable reality.

With all the knowledge I've gained—whether through classes or the guidance of mentors—I can proudly say that I am now the CEO of *"Change4Thought"*, a youth empowerment company that provides workshops and sells workbooks to inspire young people to use their voices for change. I am also the founder of *"Hustle and Flow Brunch and Socials"*, a women's empowerment event designed to create spaces for women to connect, network, and grow together. On top of that, I run *"TaijPlanned It"*, an event planning service where I help bring my clients' visions to life, creating meaningful and memorable experiences.

Each of these businesses reflects different facets of who I am: an advocate, a connector, and a visionary who believes in the transformative power of community. They allow me to continue living out my passion for making a positive impact, not just on individuals, but on entire communities. Every step I take in my journey—whether in youth empowerment, women's leadership, or event planning—is a step towards creating spaces where people can connect, thrive, and ultimately, make a difference.

My passion for helping people has driven me to organize countless events—everything from job fairs and networking events to charity drives and youth workshops. I've always felt a deep responsibility to give back, to create spaces where people can connect, learn, and grow. But behind the scenes, the journey wasn't always smooth.

There were moments when I felt incredibly low. I've had times when I felt like I was falling apart — mentally, emotionally, and spiritually. Running multiple businesses while managing a heavy workload can take its toll. I've been through periods where I felt lost, disconnected, and alone. My mental health reached its lowest point, and it became clear that I needed help. Therapy was the lifeline that I needed. It was in those therapy sessions that I learned how to love myself again. At first, I coped in unhealthy ways, through partying and distractions. But eventually, I began to find healing in more meaningful practices: I turned to God, started journaling, and took time to truly work on myself.

Learning how to balance everything and still make space for my mental health was a journey in itself. But it's one I needed to go through to become the woman I am today. I now understand the importance of taking care of myself so that I can continue to take care of others.

I share my story not to scare you, nor to pressure you into following my exact path, but to show you that entrepreneurship is a journey. It's a journey that requires commitment, perseverance, knowledge, and experience. Along the way, you'll face challenges, moments of doubt, and times when it feels like giving up would be easier. But every step of the journey—good and bad—teaches you something valuable.

Take the time you need to work on yourself. Grow, learn, and evolve. But don't forget to also invest time in working on your business. Nurture it, refine it, and give it the care it deserves. Because, just like you, your business will need to grow, adapt, and learn in order to thrive. This journey isn't a sprint; it's a marathon. And with patience, persistence, and the right mindset, you'll get there—one step at a time.

Chapter 1: Discovering Your Identity

Who are you, really?

Throughout my journey, I've struggled with finding my identity. I worked multiple jobs—everything from fast food to warehouses—and even tried my hand at different businesses. But no matter what I did, something always felt off. I couldn't quite figure out who I was or what I truly cared about. It wasn't until I took a step back and reflected that I realized much of this confusion stemmed from not truly knowing myself or understanding my core values. We all have a calling in life, but when you don't know who you are, it's hard to recognize that calling.

I had launched multiple businesses before, but none of them were successful. Why? Because I wasn't passionate about them. I was trying to build something without having a clear sense of purpose. I was starting ventures for the sake of starting them, but I didn't fully understand what drove me. I hadn't taken the time to really learn who *Taijah* was, so I couldn't create a business that I genuinely cared about.

Sometimes, finding yourself requires stepping out of your comfort zone and confronting the questions you've been avoiding. It takes real self-awareness and introspection. When I finally allowed myself that time to reflect and align with my values, everything began to fall into place. That was when I could finally create something that reflected who I was and what I stood for—a business that wasn't just about making money, but about making a difference.

What are three things you are naturally good at?

_____
_____
_____
_____
_____

What is one area in yourself where you would like to improve?

_____
_____
_____
_____
_____

What do you care about most?
(this can be an issue, a person, a place)

_____
_____
_____
_____
_____

Self Analysis

Take a moment to reflect and fill out the chart below. You can jot down your thoughts in the box, or if you prefer, use a separate piece of paper to write more. In the first box, think back to a time in your life when you felt uncertain or lost. This could be a single moment or a series of moments.

- How did you feel during this time?
- What were you experiencing or going through at that moment?

Take your time to truly reflect and be honest with yourself. This is about gaining clarity on the challenges you've faced and understanding how they've shaped your journey.

I remember there was a point in my life where I felt extremely lost. I was almost broke and in alot of debt, and I honestly didn't think there was any hope for me to get back on my feet. I felt my lowest, but I also didn't take the time to truly acknowledge the problem at the time. I can say that today I am in a much better place and that is only because I took the time to look at the problem and face it head on.

In the second box, I want you to write out your top 5 core values. These are the values that make you who you are. You need to be able to live by these values and keep these values in mind, whether you're making personal or business moves.

One value that I hold deeply is *Inclusivity*. I'm passionate about creating spaces where everyone feels welcome, valued, and heard. This belief is reflected in many of the events I organize and, more importantly, in the way I interact with people in all the spaces I occupy.

Let me share a personal example.

I recently started working at the airport as a Training and Compliance Manager. In this role, I'm responsible for training and overseeing over 500 employees. But beyond that, I'm also involved in shaping policies and making changes that impact how the workplace operates. One of the core aspects of my role is ensuring that the policies we implement foster an inclusive environment where all employees feel respected and supported. I didn't want to initially enter the space and just take over, so I decided to send out a survey first. This allowed me to hear the voices of the people who were already in the space before I went in making a bunch of changes. Whether in a large organization or a small community, *inclusivity* is at the heart of everything I do.

When you think about your Core values, it goes beyond business, think about the values that you hold close to your heart and apply them to all aspects of your life.

Self Analysis

In the bottom left box, I want you to identify your strengths. These can be personal strengths related to your business or just strengths that you have in general.

One of my strengths is that I am a connector. I can connect people with opportunities that I know will benefit them, based off having one conversation with them, or simply knowing what someone's talents and interests are.

Finally, in the bottom left box, I want you to list your weaknesses. We all have weaknesses, and that's completely okay. Just be honest and don't be afraid to be vulnerable with yourself.

Identify a period in your life when you felt uncertain or lost:	List your top 5 core values:

What are your strengths?	What are your weaknesses?

Dream Letter to Your Future Self

Write a letter to yourself 10 years from now, detailing your dreams, hopes, and what kind of person you want to be. Don't be afraid to tell yourself where you currently are right now, and what you hope to see differently 10 years from now. Be vulnerable with yourself, and take the time to analyze and reflect on what the best version of yourself will look like and write it down. Do you want to be on a better path financially? Spiritually? Mentally? What do you want for yourself 10 years from now?

Vision Board

Setting a clear vision of who you want to be in life is a big part of self-identity. I often believe that when you put things down on paper they become a reality. It's so important to *manifest* the type of person you want to be, but also truly take the time to think about what the perfect version of you looks like. Ultimately, vision boards help you clarify what you really want in life, keeping your dreams top of mind and pushing you to take tangible steps toward making them a reality.

They're more than just a collage—they're a daily reminder of the life you're working to create.

Reflecting on your dream letter to yourself and some of the questions you answered about your current identity above, I want you to create a vision board. This vision board will outline what your goals, dreams, and future will look like. This can be your vision for yourself a month from now, or a year from now, It's completely up to you.

You can draw items, or print and paste images into the pink square.

Vision Board

**After completing this chapter, take the time to reflect on some of your answers, your vision and goals.
Finding your identity will help you in the next chapter.**

Chapter 2: Finding Your Passion

I found myself burning out often because I was in spaces where I wasn't truly passionate about what I was doing. The last thing you want is to wake up every day and step into a job or run a business that doesn't fulfill you. For years, I worked in jobs I hated, but I kept pushing forward because, as many of us know, businesses aren't cheap to run, and they certainly don't run themselves.

I remember the first business I tried to start was a clothing brand. I built a beautiful website, created an Instagram page, and thought, *"Yep, this is it. This is the business that's going to take me out of Brampton."*

But let me tell you—I was humbled so quickly. I thought I had it all figured out until I had to actually stay on top of the business, engage with it, and make it sustainable. The problem was, I didn't care about it. I wasn't passionate about the clothing industry, and that lack of genuine interest made it hard to stay committed. I learned the hard way that passion is essential if you want a business to succeed. Without it, the spark just isn't there, and the drive fades fast.

If you are running a business or working a job that you don't care about, you're not going to put your best foot forward or put nearly as much effort as needed because again, you just don't care about it.

I'm not saying to quit your job and dive headfirst into your passion, but I am saying that you need to carve out time to discover what truly drives you while working in those spaces. Use those jobs as fuel to build your passion-driven business. Let the work you do now help fund the dream that's waiting for you to pursue.

Passion Brainstorm

Write down 10 things that make you happy or excited, no matter how big or small:

_____
_____
_____
_____
_____
_____
_____
_____
_____
_____

Passion Interviews

We're going to get comfortable with being uncomfortable. Your challenge is to identify three people who are passionate about what they do and reach out to them to learn about their journey. You can find these individuals on social media, through in-person connections, or by attending networking events. Don't hesitate to make the first move and ask for their insights.

Here's a sample message to help you get started:

"Hi [name], I came across your page and was inspired by your passion for [industry or field]. I'm an entrepreneur myself, and I'd love to know how you discovered your passion for what you do. Looking forward to hearing from you!"

Passion Interviews

Person 1
Name:
_____

Passion / Business:
_____

How did they discover this passion?

_____
_____
_____
_____
_____
_____
_____
_____
_____
_____
_____

Passion Interviews

Person 2
Name:
_____

Passion / Business:
_____

How did they discover this passion?

Passion Interviews

Person 3
Name:
_____

Passion / Business:
_____

How did they discover this passion?

_____
_____
_____
_____
_____
_____
_____
_____
_____

Skills vs Joys

This activity will help you identify which tasks or activities you're skilled at and enjoy, and which ones may not bring as much joy or align with your strengths. The goal is to help you discover passions that could align with your natural talents and interests.

On the *skills* side, list activities you're good at or feel confident doing. These are things where you've developed competence or expertise over time.

On the *joy* side, list activities that bring you happiness or fulfillment, even if you're not particularly skilled at them. These are things you do because they make you feel good or bring a sense of accomplishment.

Skills	**Joys**

Reflection Questions

Are there any activities that appear on both sides (things you're both good at and enjoy)?

Are there things you're skilled at but don't enjoy?

Are there activities that bring you joy, but you feel like you're not that skilled at them?

So, What Are You Passionate About?

Now that you've taken the time to reflect on your skills and joys, it's time to dive deeper into understanding your true passion.

Passion is the fuel that will keep you going when things get tough. It's what makes your work meaningful and your life fulfilling.

Chapter 3: Networking and Building Relationships

An *elevator pitch* is a short, persuasive introduction that captures attention and communicates your ideas clearly. It's something I wish I had prepared for my first networking event. But as I always say, this book is all about *GROWTH*—and we all learn as we go.

This activity is designed to help you refine your message and build confidence when introducing yourself in professional settings.

Your elevator pitch should be around 30 seconds long, and it's important to adjust it based on the context or audience you're speaking to.

The goal is to give people a snapshot of who you are, what you're passionate about, and how they can connect with you—all in a brief amount of time.

Let's dive in and try it out!

Introduction
- Start with your name.
- Hi, my name is

_____

Current Role or Title
- Briefly explain what you do or your current role.
- I am a [your job title] at [your company / organization].

_____

What You Do
- Describe what you specialize in or your main responsibilities. Example Prompt: "I focus on [describe your work / service / project]

_____
_____

Your Passion or Purpose
- Share what drives you or your mission. "I'm passionate about [your passion or cause] because [reason / impact]."

_____
_____

Unique Selling Point
- Highlight what makes you unique or what sets you apart from others. "What sets me apart is [your unique skill / experience / quality]."

_____
_____

Call to Action
- End with what you're looking for or how the listener can help you. "I would love to connect with others in [industry / field] or collaborate on [specific project or interest]."

_____
_____

Putting It All Together

Combine your responses from the prompts to form a cohesive *elevator pitch*.

Example Elevator Pitch:

Hi, my name is Taijah Cox-Armstrong. I'm the CEO of Change4Thought. I focus on empowering youth through sports and educational initiatives. I'm passionate about teaching inclusivity because I believe everyone deserves a chance to thrive. What sets me apart is my ability to connect diverse communities through impactful events. I would love to connect with others in the non-profit sector or collaborate on initiatives aimed at youth empowerment.

Important Note:

Did you notice that I didn't include all of my businesses? It's important to share the correct information with the correct person and to tweak your *elevator pitch* depending on the space you're in.

Write your Elevator Pitch Below:

After completing this chapter, take the time to reflect on some of your answers, your vision and goals. Finding your identity will help you in the next chapter.

Social Media Networking Challenge

Networking doesn't have to happen just in person at events—it can also take place online through social media. While building relationships on social platforms may take a bit more time, it can have a significant impact on expanding your network.

I always recommend starting by engaging with someone's content before reaching out directly. Take the time to like their posts, leave thoughtful comments, or interact with their stories over time. This builds familiarity and trust before you make your initial contact.

Pick one platform—whether it's LinkedIn, Instagram, or another—and commit to engaging with at least five new connections each week. This can include liking their posts, commenting on content, or even sending a direct message.

Be sure to document your interactions and track any new opportunities that come from these engagements. You'll be surprised at how these small, consistent actions can lead to meaningful connections and growth in your network.

Platform:

_____

Date of Social Media Interaction:

_____

Social Media handle of the person you interacted with:

_____

Type of interaction:
(check all that apply)

☐ Like
☐ Comment
☐ Share
☐ DM

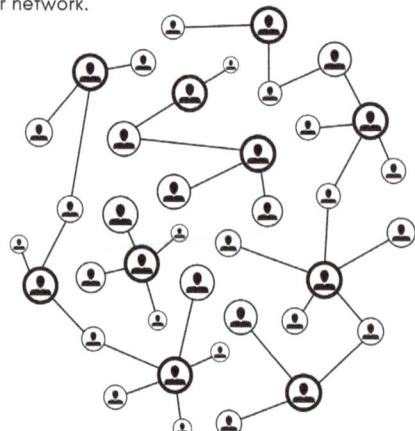
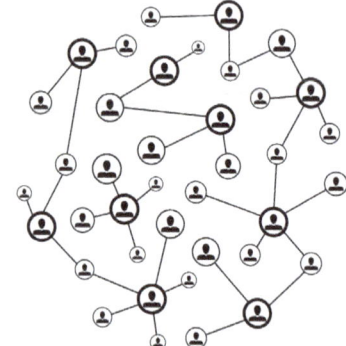

Social Media Networking Challenge

Platform:

_____

Date of Social Media Interaction:

_____

Social Media handle of the person you interacted with:

_____

Type of interaction: Check all that Apply

- ☐ Like
- ☐ Comment
- ☐ Share
- ☐ DM

Social Media Networking Challenge

Platform:

_____

Date of Social Media Interaction:

_____

Social Media handle of the person you interacted with:

_____

Type of interaction: Check all that Apply

- ☐ Like
- ☐ Comment
- ☐ Share
- ☐ DM

Social Media Networking Challenge

Platform:

_____

Date of Social Media Interaction:

_____

Social Media handle of the person you interacted with:

_____

Type of interaction: Check all that Apply

☐ Like
☐ Comment
☐ Share
☐ DM

Social Media Networking Challenge

Platform:

_____

Date of Social Media Interaction:

_____

Social Media handle of the person you interacted with:

_____

Type of interaction: Check all that Apply

- [ ] Like
- [ ] Comment
- [ ] Share
- [ ] DM

Challenge

The **GOAL** of this challenge is to encourage you to attend a networking event and actively engage with others in your industry or area of interest. By stepping out of your comfort zone, you'll build valuable connections that can aid you in both your personal and professional life.

Start by researching upcoming networking events in your area—these could be conferences, workshops, meetups, or social gatherings. Use platforms like *Eventbrite*, *Meetup*, *LinkedIn*, or *Social Media* to find events that resonate with your interests.

Once you've found an event, register and make a commitment to attend.

Take a moment to jot down your goals for the experience. What do you hope to achieve? Perhaps you want to meet new people, learn about a specific topic, or find a mentor. Also, practice your elevator pitch!

Reflection

Reflecting on past networking experiences can provide valuable insights and help participants identify areas for improvement.

This activity encourages self-awareness and growth.

Reflect on the recent networking event you attended. What went well? What could I have done differently? and What did I learn?

Journal your thoughts and create an action plan for future networking events.

Chapter 4: Money Management for Entrepreneurs

As we all know, it takes money to make money, and running a business is not cheap! But here's the thing—we're human, and it's important to take the time to reflect on your finances and start budgeting accordingly. As I've mentioned before, I worked multiple jobs to fund my business. I worked long, gruelling shifts in warehouses, sometimes over 12 hours, late into the night. But I did it because I knew it was necessary to fund the life I wanted to build for myself.

I used to be terrified of finances. I avoided looking at my numbers because it would literally give me a headache. But ladies, let me tell you—please, do not be like the old me! Take the time to educate yourself and maintain financial health.

For a while, I was drowning in debt from some poor financial decisions I made. I had two credit cards maxed out when I was in university, and I was spending way more money than I was bringing in. The wake-up call came when I found myself sitting in the negatives, unsure how I was going to put gas in my car or pay the next bill. I was living pay cheque to pay cheque, calculating what I could spend before my pay cheque even came in. That was when I realized I had to change my relationship with money.

I knew exactly where I had gone wrong financially, and today, I can proudly say I'm in a much better place. It took time, but I made the decision to not only look at where I went wrong but also to figure out how to improve. I started by paying off my debts, and eventually, I learned how to invest my money so that it could grow while I was working—or while I continued building my businesses.

This chapter will help you dive into your financial story, reflect on where you can improve, and start building a healthier relationship with your finances.

Your Money Story

Journaling has always been a powerful tool for me to reflect on different aspects of life.

Now, I want you to take some time to really dive deep and explore your relationship with money.

- Where are you struggling?
- In what areas do you need more support?
- How did you get to this point in your financial journey?

Be honest with yourself as you reflect—this is your opportunity to better understand your finances and uncover what needs to change.

Journal Prompt:

What's your relationship with money like?
Is it healthy?
Have you had low periods?
Where do you struggle most?

30 Day Expense Tracking Challenge

For the next 30 days, track every single expense, no matter how small!

Date	Description Groceries, night out with the girls, savings etc.	Amount Spent	Category Essentials, wants, savings etc

30 Day Expense Tracking Challenge

For the next 30 days, track every single expense, no matter how small!

Date	Description Groceries, night out with the girls, savings etc.	Amount Spent	Category Essentials, wants, savings etc

30 Day Expense Tracking Challenge

For the next 30 days, track every single expense, no matter how small!

Date	Description Groceries, night out with the girls, savings etc.	Amount Spent	Category Essentials, wants, savings etc

At the END of your 30 days, reflect on your spending patterns. Write a paragraph about what you learned.

Chapter 5: Starting and Scaling Your Business

Starting my business the right way was one of the toughest challenges I faced on my entrepreneurial journey. At first, I didn't know much about the business world—I just had a passion and a product. My first big mistake was thinking I could jump straight into selling without doing any research. The last thing you want is to be asked a question about your product or service, and not have a clue what the answer is.

I also didn't have a clear understanding of who my target audience was, nor did I have a brand that aligned with the goals of my business. Before Change4Thought, I was simply selling my books. My book cover was brown, and I chose that colour because I liked the different shades of brown—not because it represented the brand or the mission I wanted to build.

After a while, I started asking myself, *"Why aren't my sales as high as I expected?"* And the answer was clear:

I hadn't put enough time, research, or strategy into my business or product.

That's when I decided to enroll in a business class. There, I learned how to properly start and structure my business, how to build a strong foundation, and eventually how to scale it to reach its full potential.

As I dove deeper into what I wanted *"I Will Make a Difference"* to become, *"Change4Thought"* took shape. I developed a brand identity, built a community, and focused on creating something that was sustainable. Today, *Change4Thought* is forming strong, lasting partnerships with school boards and non-profit organizations.

If you want your business to succeed, you need to take the time to figure out what it stands for.

Ask yourself:

"Who are you trying to connect with?" and "What message are you trying to communicate?"

Taking the time to define these things early on will give your business a clearer direction and a stronger chance of growth.

Create a Business Plan

Creating a business plan will allow you to take the time to truly learn about your business and who it will serve.

This part of the book is simply a guide to help you create a base for your business plan. Your business plan may change as the goals for your business change.

Complete the business plan below for your personal business.

Sample Problem: Change4Thought

THE PROBLEM

- Currently there are not enough expanded learning tools available to educators, parents, and youth organization groups that teach kids about anti-racism
- Youth are being exposed to the world around them everyday but are not given the tools to successfully combat this world
- Current anti-racism children's books are only story telling books, there's no expanded learning books that follow a textbook/workbook format for youth ages 7-15.

What is the problem your business is trying to solve?

Sample Solution:

THE SOLUTION

- We offer workshops and programs that teachers and youth groups can utilize to expand anti-racism learning in their classrooms
- Our workshops teaches youth about the world around them and the part that they play in this world.
- Through our expanded learning workbook-lets and workshops we offer the opportunity for youth ages 7-15, to engage in meaningful activity's which teach them about topics such as Equity vs Equality, Identity, Power, Racism, Using their voice, and the difference they can make in the world.

How is your business the solution to this problem?

Sample About Us Statement: Change4Thought

Change4Thought facilitates educational, expanded learning programs that enrich school curricula.

Our focus revolves around the critical topic of inclusivity, diversity, racism, leadership and empowering children to make positive changes in the world.

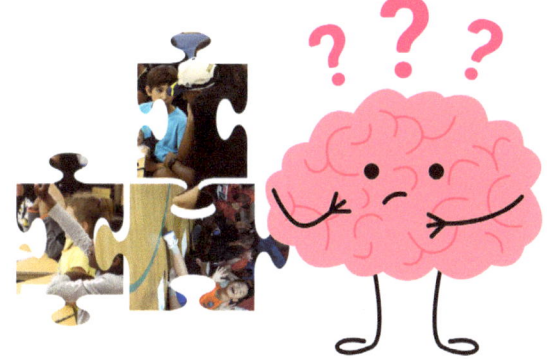

What is your businesses About Us Statement?

Sample Target Market: Change4Thought

MARKET DESCRIPTION

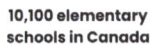

10,100 elementary schools in Canada

Parents

350 youth organizations in Canada

Who is your Target Market?

_____
_____
_____
_____
_____
_____
_____
_____
_____
_____
_____
_____
_____
_____
_____

Sample Competition: Change4Thought

COMPETITION

25 POPULAR FREELANCE YOUTH SPEAKERS (ALL ADULTS)
3 OTHER YOUTH-LED SPEAKING ORGANIZATIONS IN ONTARIO

HOW ARE WE DIFFERENT?
THE ONLY PUBLISHED CHILDREN'S ANTI-RACISM ACTIVITY BOOKLET ON THE MARKET
WE INCORPORATE A LEARNING TOOL (OUR BOOKS) IN OUR WORKSHOPS AND MANY OTHER ORGANIZATIONS DON'T HAVE THEIR OWN LEARNING TOOL APART FROM THEIR
WORKSHOPS
WORKSHOPS ARE DONE THROUGH A BY YOUTH, FOR YOUTH VISION, OUR FACILITATOR
IS UNDER THE AGE OF 25 THEREFORE, EASILY RELATABLE FOR THE KIDS
WE OFFER AN E-LEARNING ONLINE MODULE THAT SCHOOLS CAN PURCHASE FOR A SELF-GUIDED LEARNING OPPORTUNITY

Who is your Competition?

Sample Marketing Strategies: Change4Thought

MARKETING STRATEGIES

Marketing Channel	Description
Social Media (Instagram, Facebook, Twitter)	Utilizing various social media platforms like Instagram, Facebook, and Twitter.
Boots on the Ground Marketing	Handing out flyers to principals and guidance counselors at elementary schools.
Conferences/ Events	Attending teachers' conferences to promote our products/services.

How will you Market your business?

_____
_____
_____
_____
_____
_____
_____
_____
_____
_____
_____
_____
_____
_____
_____
_____
_____
_____

Sample Financial Breakdown: Change4Thought

FINANCIAL BREAKDOWN

Product/Service	Price	Cost of Printing	Profit
Stitched Bound Books	$25.99		
Spiral Bound Books	$30.99		
Lesson Plans (Physical)	$13.99		
Workshops	$350 flat per 90 min		

Please fill in the chart below:

Product / Service	Price	Cost for YOU	Profit

Sample Contact: Change4Thought

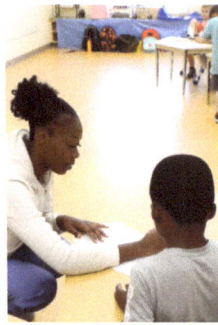

- 🌐 www.change4thought.com
- 📞 647-721-0028
- 📷 @change4thought_
- ✉ change4thought@gmail.com

How should people Contact you?

Create a Brand Identity

Creating your brand idea is key to understanding what your brand will represent, and what the face of your brand will look like. Your brand identity is the first thing that comes to mind when people think of your brand.

What do you want people to feel when they see your brand?

Your logo needs to be clean and clear, this will be the first impression you are making on the people who will be connecting with your brand. In order to come up with a meaningful logo, you need to figure out what message you are trying to send to your audience, take the time to also look at the logos of your competitors.

What Message is your brand trying to convey?

What is your Vision / Mission?

Sample Vision/ Mission Statement: Change4Thought

TO EMPOWER YOUTH THROUGH INTERACTIVE WORKSHOPS, AND RESOURCES AND PROVIDE THEM WITH THE TOOLS THEY NEED TO CREATE POSITIVE CHANGE IN THEIR COMMUNITIES.

OUR VISION

WE AIM TO INSPIRE A GENERATION OF YOUNG LEADERS WHO ARE PASSIONATE ABOUT MAKING A DIFFERENCE. WE BELIEVE THAT BY AMPLIFYING THEIR VOICES, WE CAN CREATE A MORE INCLUSIVE, EQUITABLE, AND SUSTAINABLE FUTURE FOR ALL.

What is your Mission / Vision?

_____
_____
_____
_____
_____
_____
_____
_____
_____
_____

Sample Logo: Change4Thought

Versions of our logo can be used to match a variety of materials and applications. Make sure to apply them appropriately.

Sketch and plan out a rough logo on the next page

Using the box below, sketch and plan out a LOGO for your business:

After completing this chapter, take the time to reflect on some of your answers, your vision and goals.
Finding your identity will help you in the next chapter.

Sample Typography: Change4Thought

Take some time to play around on Word, Adobe, or Canva, to figure out what you want your Brand Fonts to look like. Are you going for a more elegant look? Or playful?

List 3-5 Fonts that you like for your brand

Colour Palette

Identifying your brand's colour palette is essential for reflecting its identity and personality.

The colours you choose should align with the message you want to communicate.

For example, if you're aiming for a more professional or serious tone, darker, more muted colours might be the right choice. On the other hand, if your brand is geared toward children or a fun, playful audience, brighter, more vibrant colours can help convey that energy.

The right colour palette not only makes your brand visually appealing, but also reinforces the emotions and values you want your audience to associate with it.

Sample Brand Colours: Change4Thought

Using Canva, play around with the Colour Palettes. What colors connect with you and your brand the most?

_____
_____
_____
_____
_____
_____

List Colour Codes:

_____
_____
_____
_____
_____
_____

Reasons why you chose these colours:

_____
_____
_____
_____
_____
_____
_____

Scaling Your Business

Scaling your business can feel like a daunting task, but one of the most effective ways I've learned to scale is through *partnerships*.

Partnerships offer the opportunity to connect with other businesses, brands, or organizations that share similar goals and values.

When you form strategic alliances, you can pool resources, expand your reach, and collaborate on initiatives that benefit both parties.

Take a moment to reflect on potential partners who could help you scale your business. These could be local organizations, other small businesses, or even larger corporate brands that align with your mission.

Use Google, Instagram and LinkedIn to help you answer the questions:

Name of business, contact information and why you want to connect with them:

_____
_____
_____
_____
_____

Name of business, contact information and why you want to connect with them:

_____
_____
_____
_____
_____

Name of business, contact information and why you want to connect with them:

_____
_____
_____
_____
_____

Name of business, contact information and why you want to connect with them:

_____
_____
_____
_____

Name of business, contact information and why you want to connect with them:

_____
_____
_____
_____

Name of business, contact information and why you want to connect with them:

_____
_____
_____
_____
_____
_____

Name of business, contact information and why you want to connect with them:

_____
_____
_____
_____

Name of business, contact information and why you want to connect with them:

_____
_____
_____
_____

Once you've completed your list, choose one potential partner you'd like to reach out to first.

Ask yourself: What value can you bring to this partner?

You already know why you want to connect with them, but now think about what benefits they will gain by partnering with you and your brand. How can you offer something that will be valuable to them, whether it's exposure, resources, or a shared mission? This will help you approach the partnership from a place of mutual benefit, which is key to building a strong, successful relationship.

Chapter 6: Self-Care

Self-care was something I used to completely overlook. I didn't really prioritize it or even think much about it. I believed that in order to be successful, I always needed to be on the go, 24/7. If I wasn't making some kind of business move or working on a new venture, I felt like I wasn't doing enough. And, as you can probably guess, that mentality led to constant burnout. There were days I wouldn't eat because I was jumping from work to a workshop to a call. There were days I'd fall behind on my schoolwork simply because I couldn't find the balance.

It wasn't until I saw the impact on both my physical and mental health that I truly began to take self-care seriously.

I want to emphasize just how crucial it is to take care of yourself, because your business needs the best version of you in order to thrive.

For me, self-care looks different depending on the day. Sometimes it's enjoying a meal with friends; other times, it's as simple as curling up with my favourite comfort show on a quiet Sunday afternoon. The point is, you need to make time to relax and recharge. Put as much energy into taking care of yourself as you put into growing your business.

You can't pour from an empty cup.

Self-care isn't a luxury—it's a necessity for both your well-being and the success of your business.

Create a Personal Self-Care Plan

I encourage you to take time to create a personal self-care plan that addresses the following four key areas:

Mental, Emotional, Physical, and Spiritual.

While it's common to focus on just one of these areas, true well-being comes from nurturing all of them. By considering each aspect of self-care, you'll be better equipped to show up as your best self.

An Example of My Self-Care Plan:

- **Mental**: Read a chapter of a self-help book before bed.
- **Emotional**: Write in my gratitude journal every morning.
- **Physical**: Go to the gym at least 2x a week.
- **Spiritual**: Pray every morning and every night and thank God for the day he has given me.

Your Self-Care Plan:

- **Mental**:

_____
_____
_____
_____
_____

- **Emotional:**

  _____
  _____
  _____
  _____
  _____
  _____
  _____

- **Physical:**

  _____
  _____
  _____
  _____
  _____
  _____
  _____

- **Spiritual:**

  _____
  _____
  _____
  _____
  _____
  _____
  _____

- **Share Any Additional Discoveries:**

  _____
  _____
  _____
  _____
  _____

Gratitude Journal

Taking the time to reflect on the things you're grateful for is a great way to boost your mental health. Sometimes we don't take the time to acknowledge and appreciate the good things that are happening in our life because we're so focused on the negatives.

Prompt #1 : Who is a person you are grateful for?

thankful

Gratitude Journal

Prompt #2 : What is a challenge you've overcome that you now feel grateful for?

thankful

Gratitude Journal

Prompt #3: What is something about yourself that you are proud of and grateful for?

thankful

Gratitude Journal

Prompt #4 : What is a skill or talent you have that you're thankful for?

thankful

Challenge

I want to challenge you to take a personal day to yourself, pick a self care activity from the list below and document how it went.

- [ ] Get a massage
- [ ] Get a mani / pedi
- [ ] Take a class
- [ ] Read a book

- [ ] Buy yourself a gift
- [ ] Meditate
- [ ] Take a fitness class
- [ ] Other

Self-care
IS EMPOWERMENT

Date of activity: _____

What did you decide to do? _____

How did it go / how do you feel after completing this activity?

_____
_____
_____
_____
_____
_____
_____
_____
_____

Message from Taijah

I hope this book helped you discover more about yourself, understand the deeper meaning behind your business, and connect with your true purpose. Remember, many of these insights will come with experience. No matter how much you write down or plan, it's up to you to take action and bring your journal entries, business plan, and personal goals to life.

Only you can do the work necessary to make yourself successful. Without the right mindset and drive, progress will be hard to achieve. Take my story as a guide—learn from it, and see what resonates with you. Not every exercise in this book may feel relevant to where you are right now, and that's okay. Don't be afraid to revisit certain activities as you grow and evolve in the months or years ahead.

It took me years to find my passion, my voice, and my path, and even now, I'm not fully satisfied. There's always more room for growth, more opportunities to improve, and a new version of myself to strive for. The journey of self-improvement is ongoing, but it requires self-reflection, action, and a willingness to embrace change.

To all the hustlers, dreamers, and go-getters—keep going. One day, all your hard work will pay off.

Taijah Cox-Armstrong

Come Join Us At Our Next Hustle and Flow Brunch and Networking Event! We Can't Wait to See You There!

@ HNF.SOCIAL

Come Join Us At Our Next Hustle and Flow Brunch and Networking Event! We Can't Wait to See You There!

HNF.SOCIAL